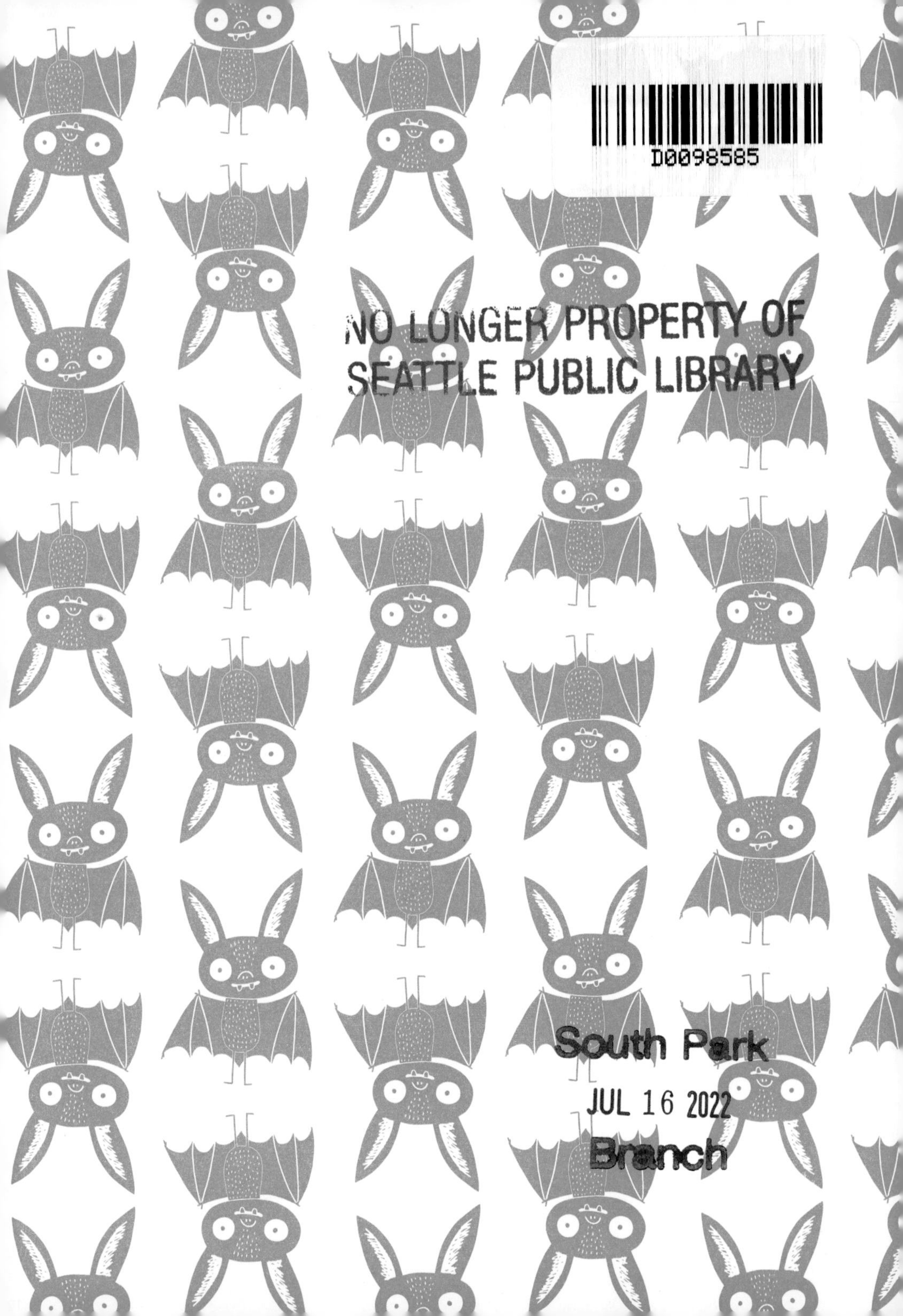

THE BAT

Tundra Books, an imprint of Penguin Random House Canada Young Readers, a Penguin Random House Company

Library and Archives Canada Cataloguing in Publication

Title: The bat / Elise Gravel.
Other titles: Chauve-souris. English
Names: Gravel, Elise, author.
Series: Gravel, Elise. Petits dégoûtants. English.
Description: Series statement: Disgusting critters | Translation of: La chauve-souris.
Identifiers: Canadiana (print) 20190141743 | Canadiana (ebook) 20190141786 | ISBN 9780735266483 (hardcover) | ISBN 9780735266490 (EPUB)
Subjects: LCSH: Bats—Juvenile literature.
Classification: LCC QL737.C5 G7213 2020 | DDC j599.4—dc23

Published simultaneously in the United States of America by Tundra Books of Northern New York, an imprint of Penguin Random House Canada Young Readers, a Penguin Random House Company

Library of Congress Control Number: 2019944417

English edition edited by Samantha Swenson
Designed by Elise Gravel and Tundra Books
The artwork in this book was rendered digitally.

Printed and bound in China

www.penguinrandomhouse.ca

1 2 3 4 5   24 23 22 21 20

Penguin
Random House
tundra | TUNDRA BOOKS

Elise Gravel

THE BAT

WHAT'S UP?

tundra

Dear friends, I'd like to present the

CHIROPTERA.

That's his scientific name.

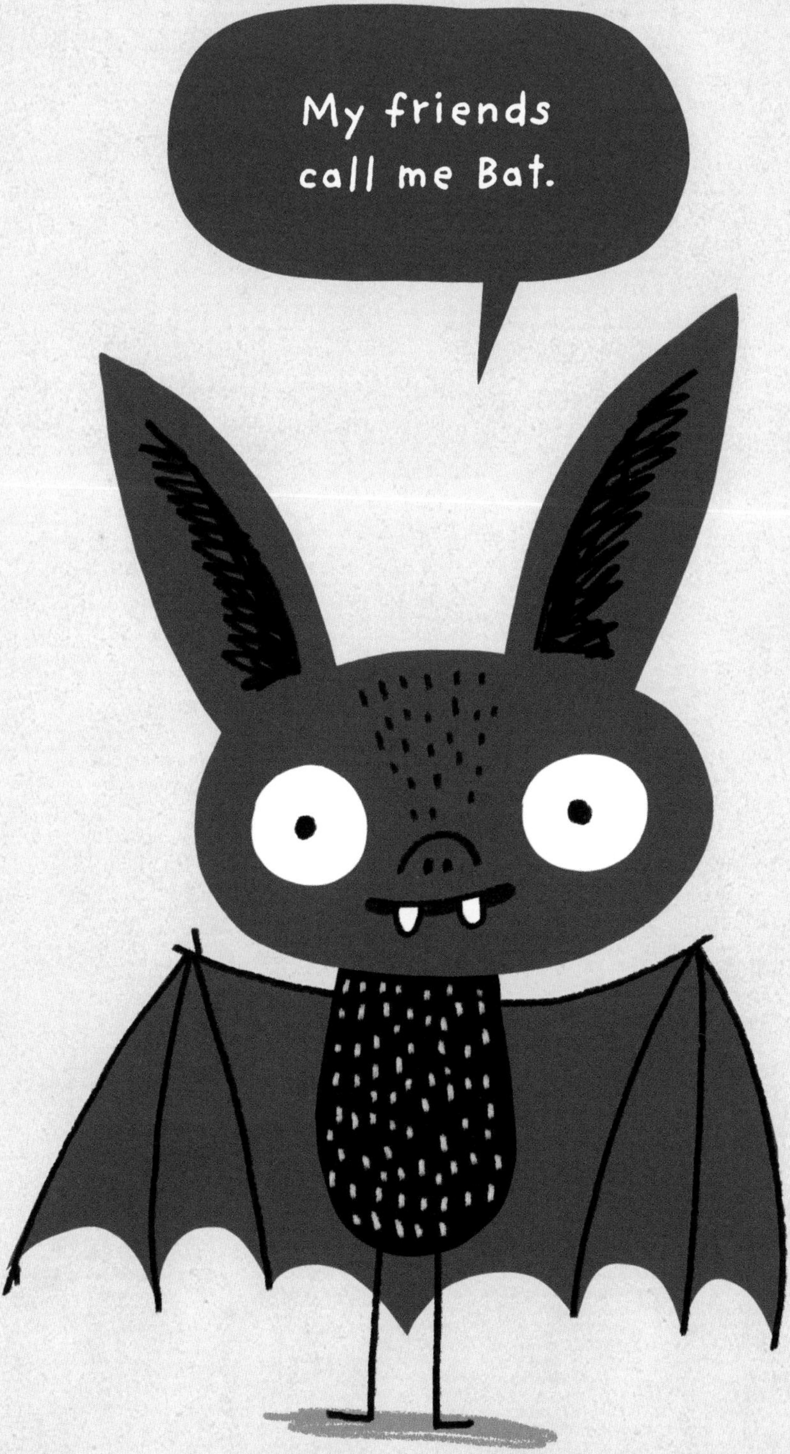
My friends call me Bat.

The bat is the only mammal that can

FLY,

even though some other mammals can glide.

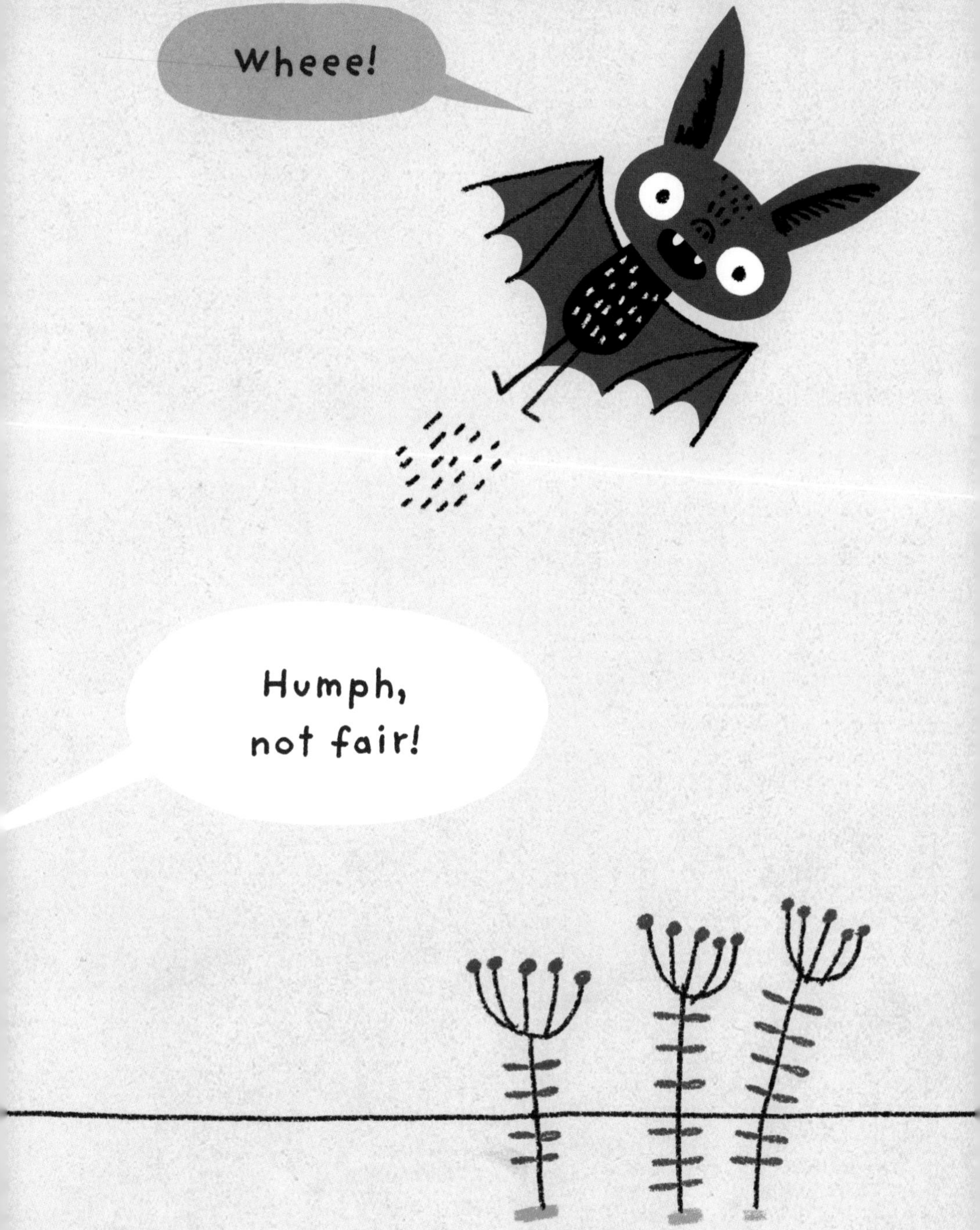
Wheee!
Humph, not fair!

Chiro comes from an ancient Greek word that means "hand" and *ptera* comes from a word that means "wing." The word *chiroptera* tells us that the bat's hands are used as

WINGS.

These stems are his

FINGERS.

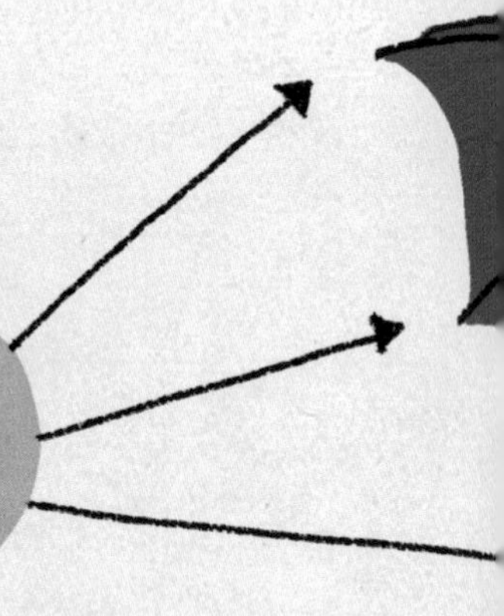

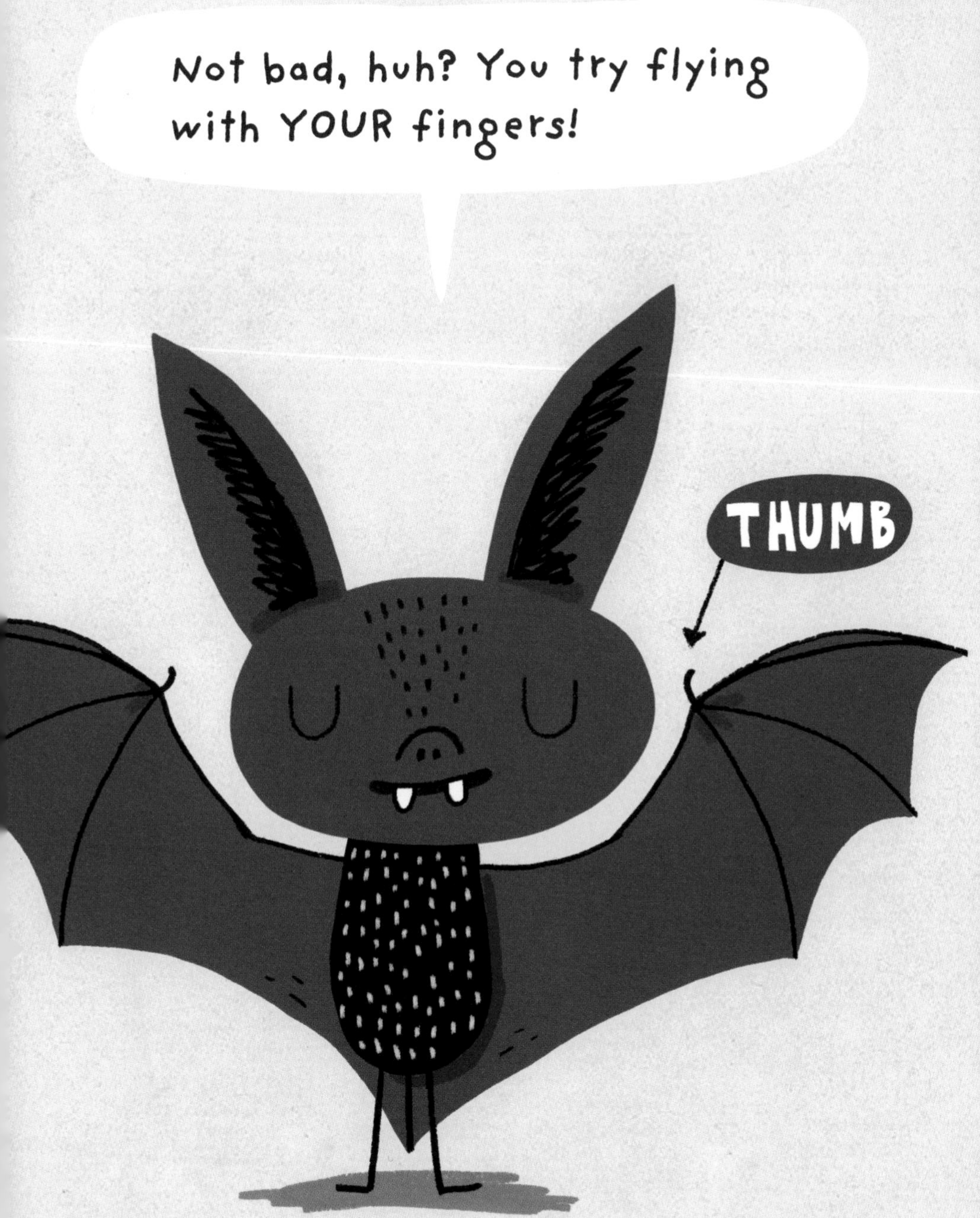
Not bad, huh? You try flying with YOUR fingers!
THUMB

There are more than

1,200

species of bats. The smallest measures about 1.2 inches, or 3 centimeters. The largest can measure up to 5.5 feet, or 1.7 meters, from wing tip to wing tip.

Good things come
in small packages.

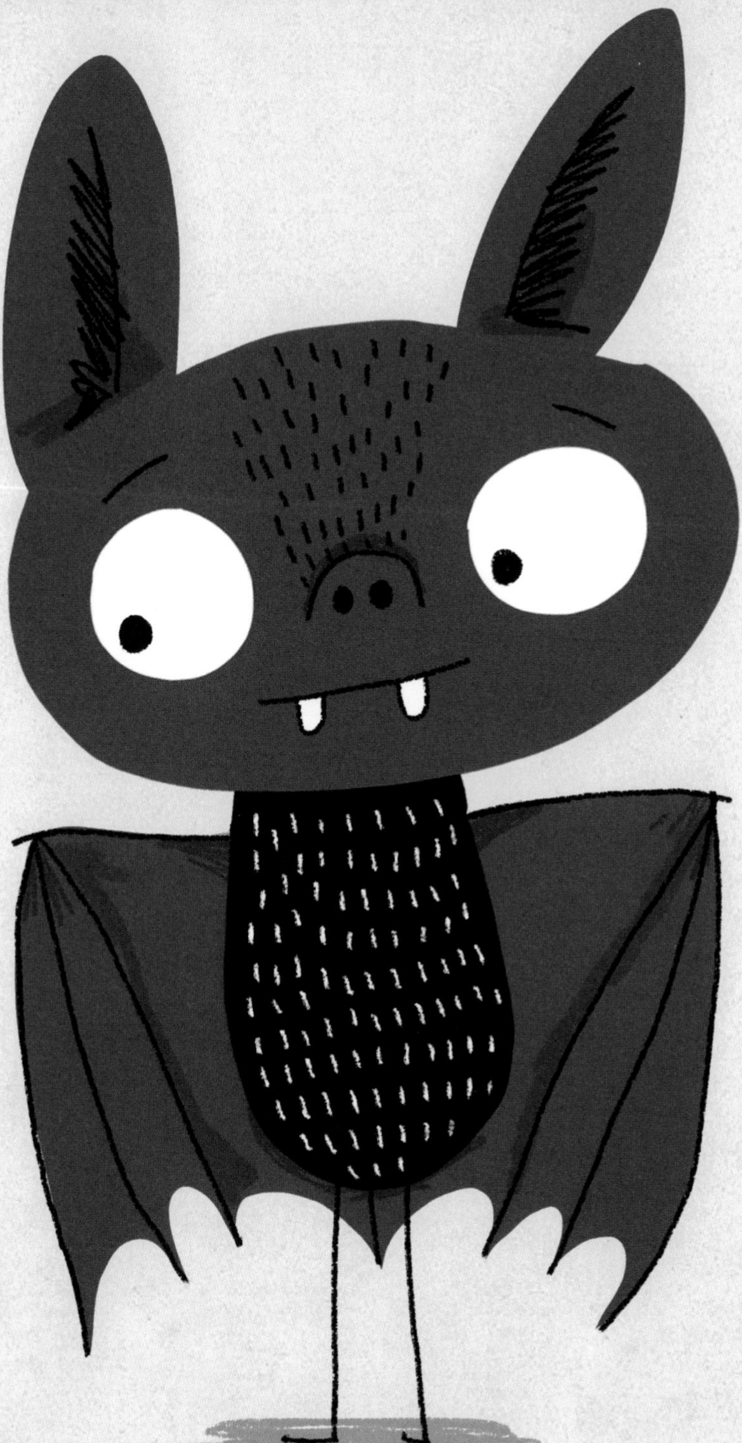

The bat is found pretty much everywhere around the world except in places that are very

COLD.

I'm not really a fan of winter sports.

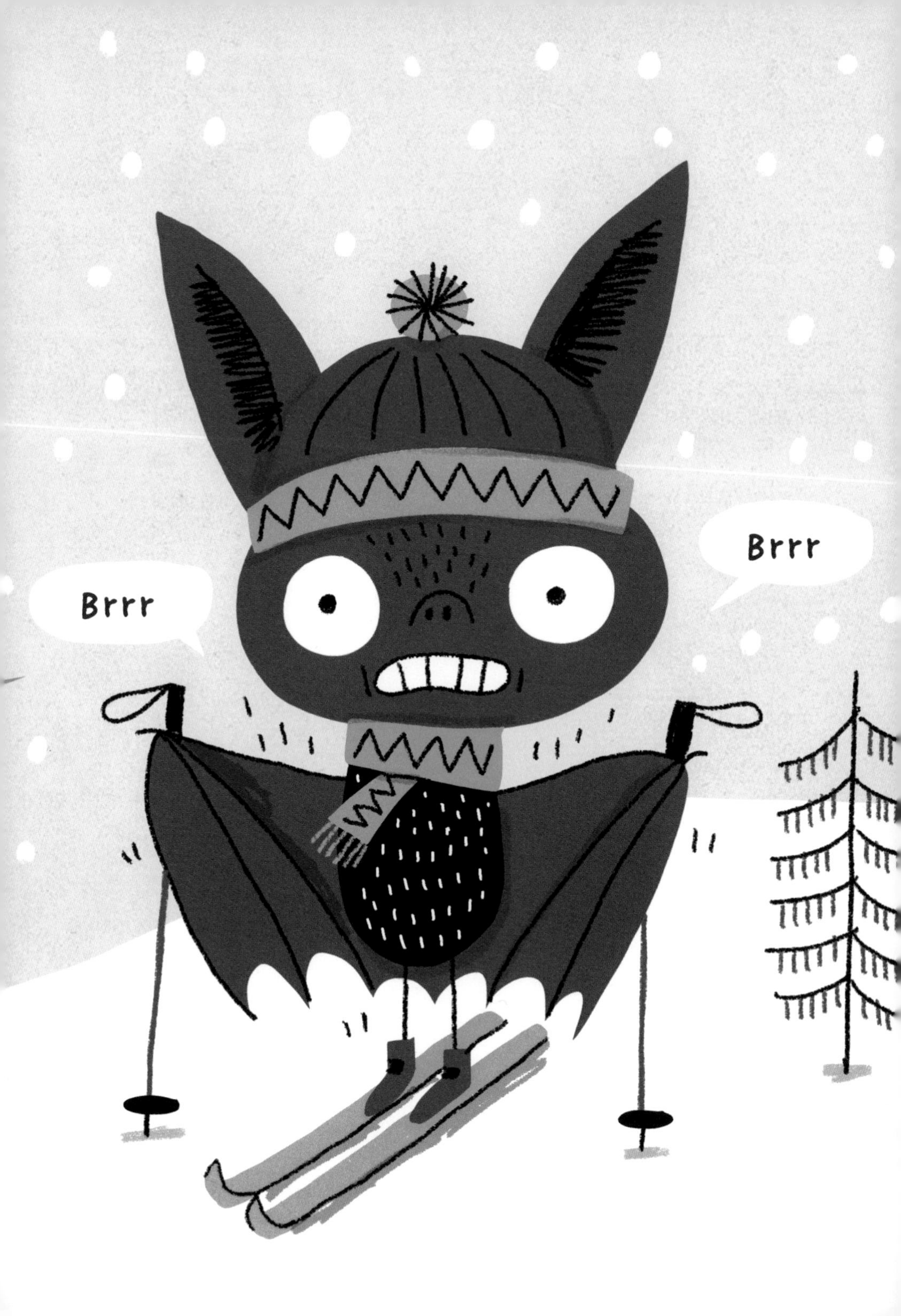
Brrr
Brrr

Most bats feed on

INSECTS.

AHHHH!

Others prefer to eat fruit.

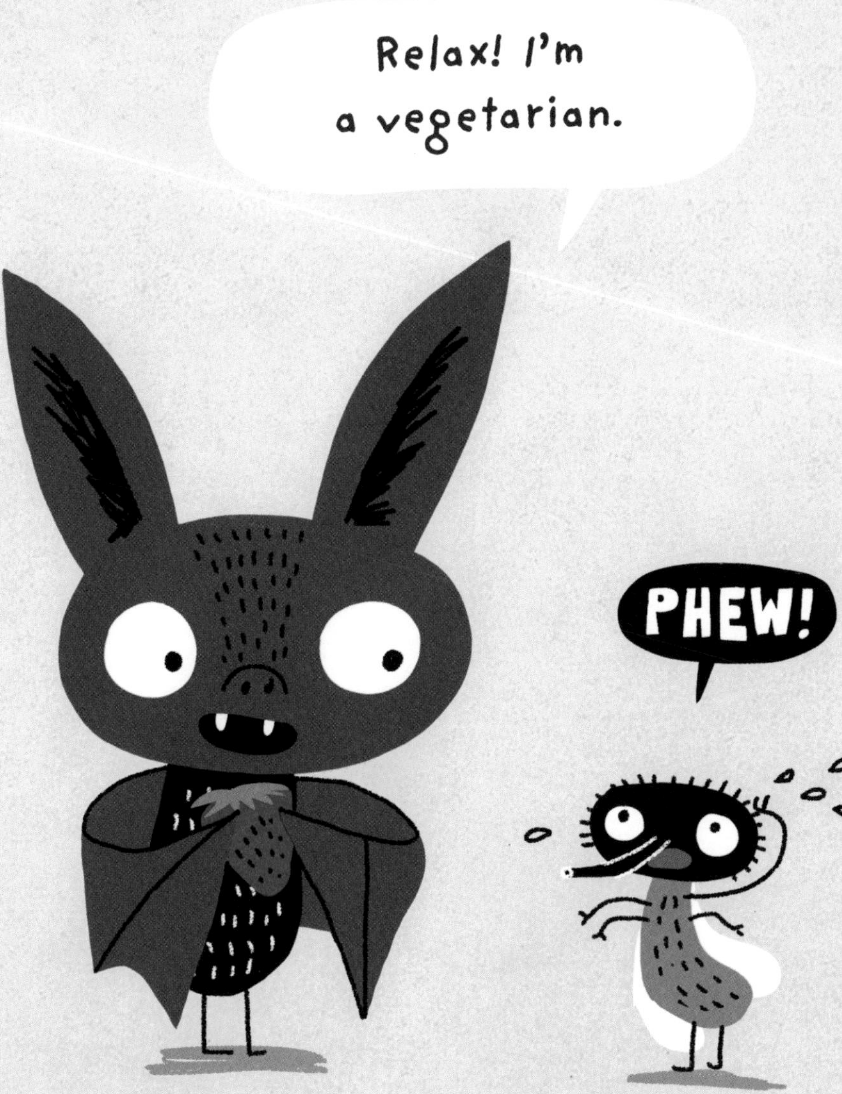
Relax! I'm
a vegetarian.
PHEW!

Some feed on small animals, and some bats can even fish!

The bat lives in large groups and finds shelter in places like caves, trees and the roofs of houses. He prefers to go out at night and rest during the day. He sleeps hanging

UPSIDE
DOWN.

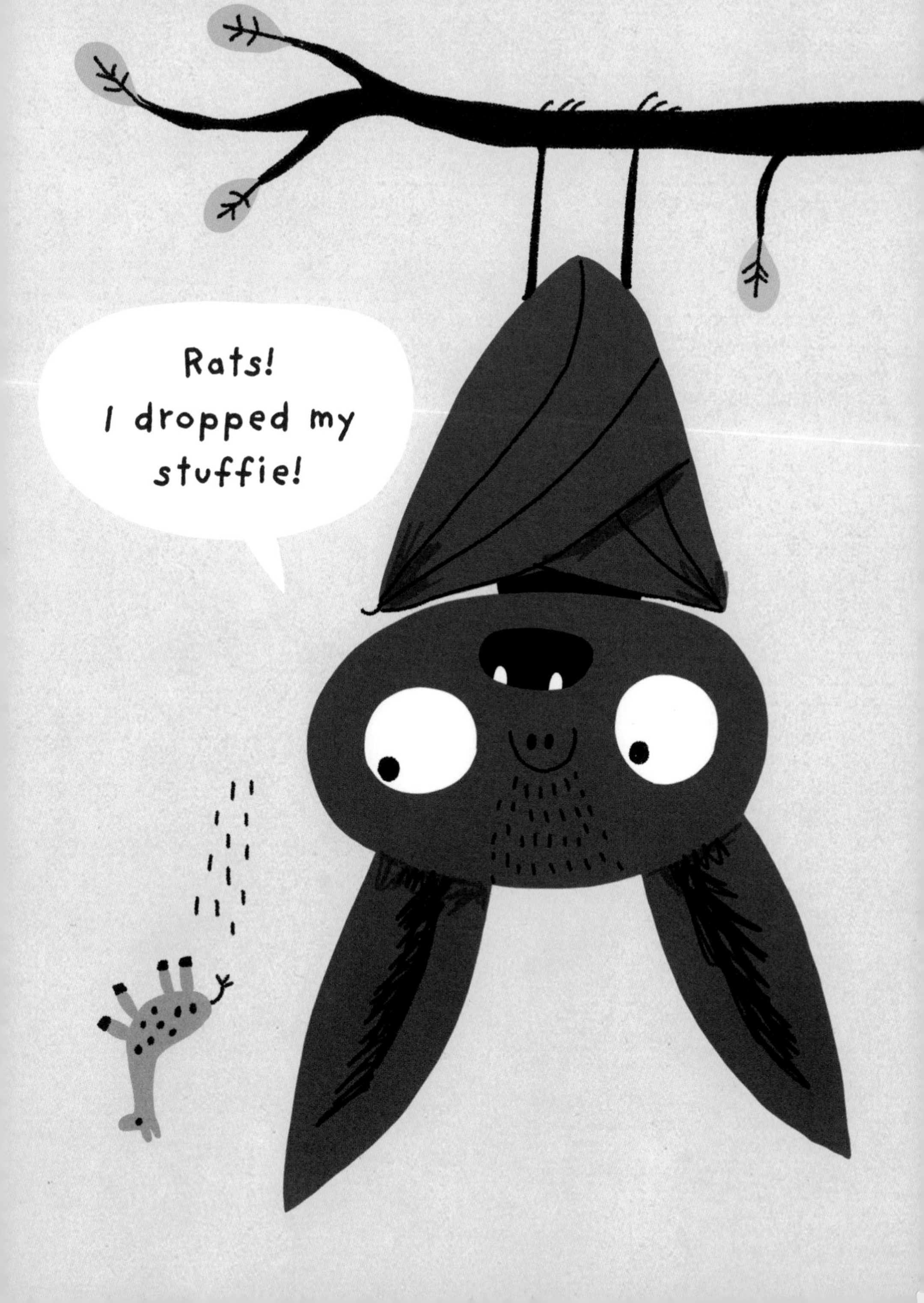
Rats!
I dropped my
stuffie!

In winter, the bat

HIBERNATES.

He lowers his body temperature, which allows him to sleep while saving energy all winter long.

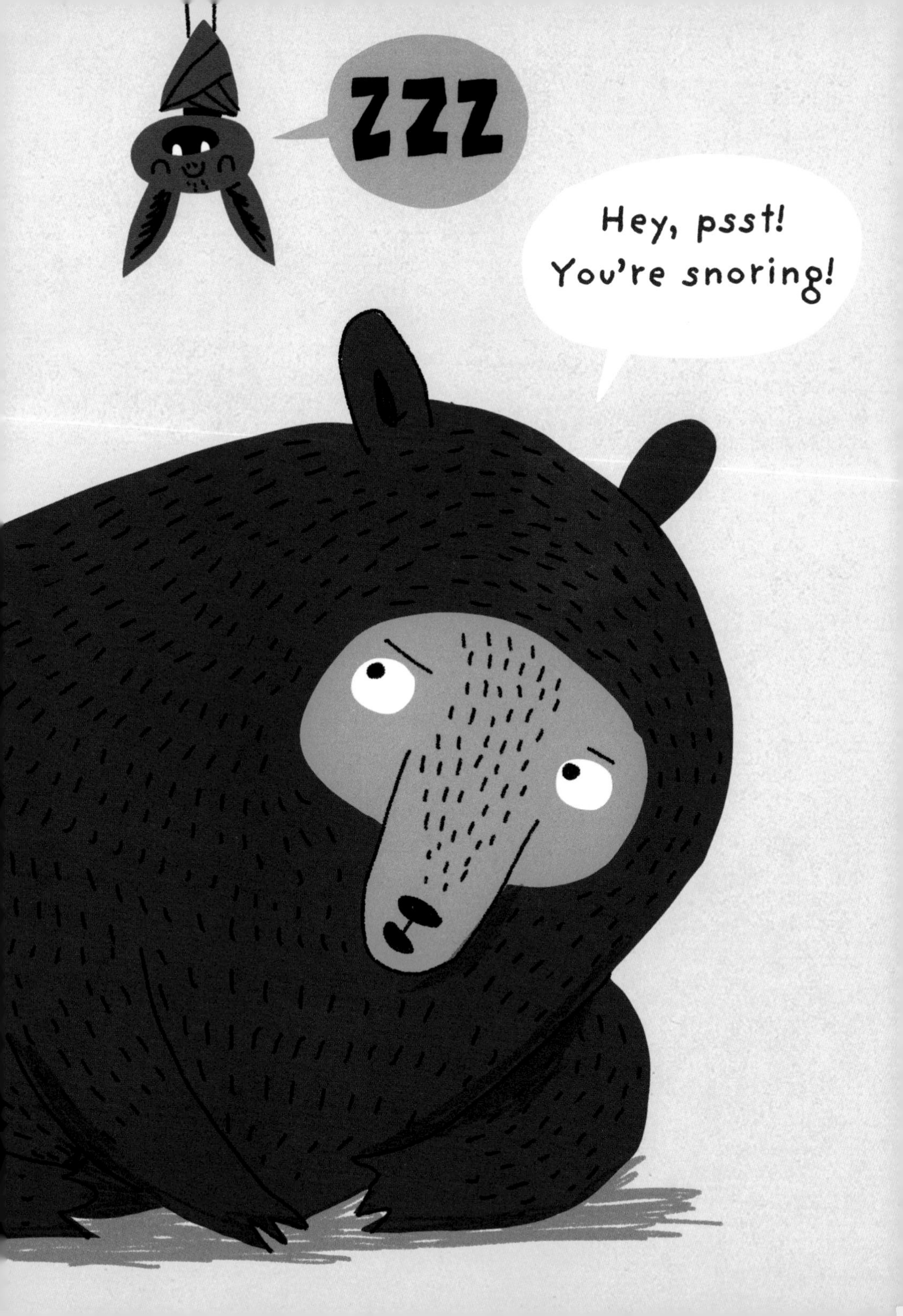
ZZZ
Hey, psst! You're snoring!

Since the bat is a

MAMMAL,

the female does not lay eggs. She gives birth to one or two babies. Baby bats can fly when they are a month old.

Mama, look! Me fly! Me fly!

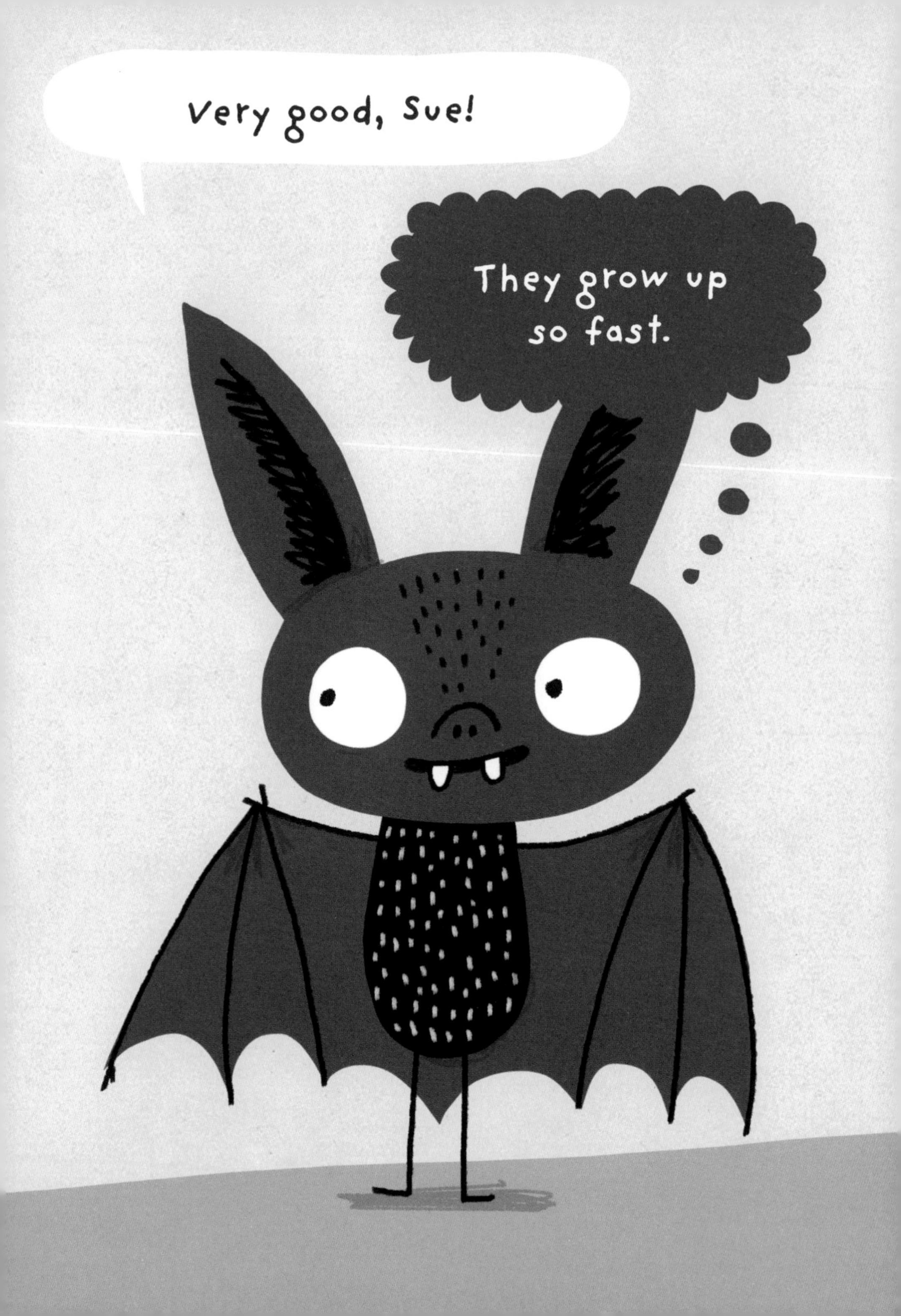
Very good, Sue!
They grow up so fast.

Many bats use

ECHOLOCATION

to find their way around. They "throw" sound vibrations that bounce off things around them. The sound vibrations come back to the bats' ears and tell them if there is an obstacle in their way. Thanks to this pretty cool ability, bats can capture prey at night and fly in the dark.

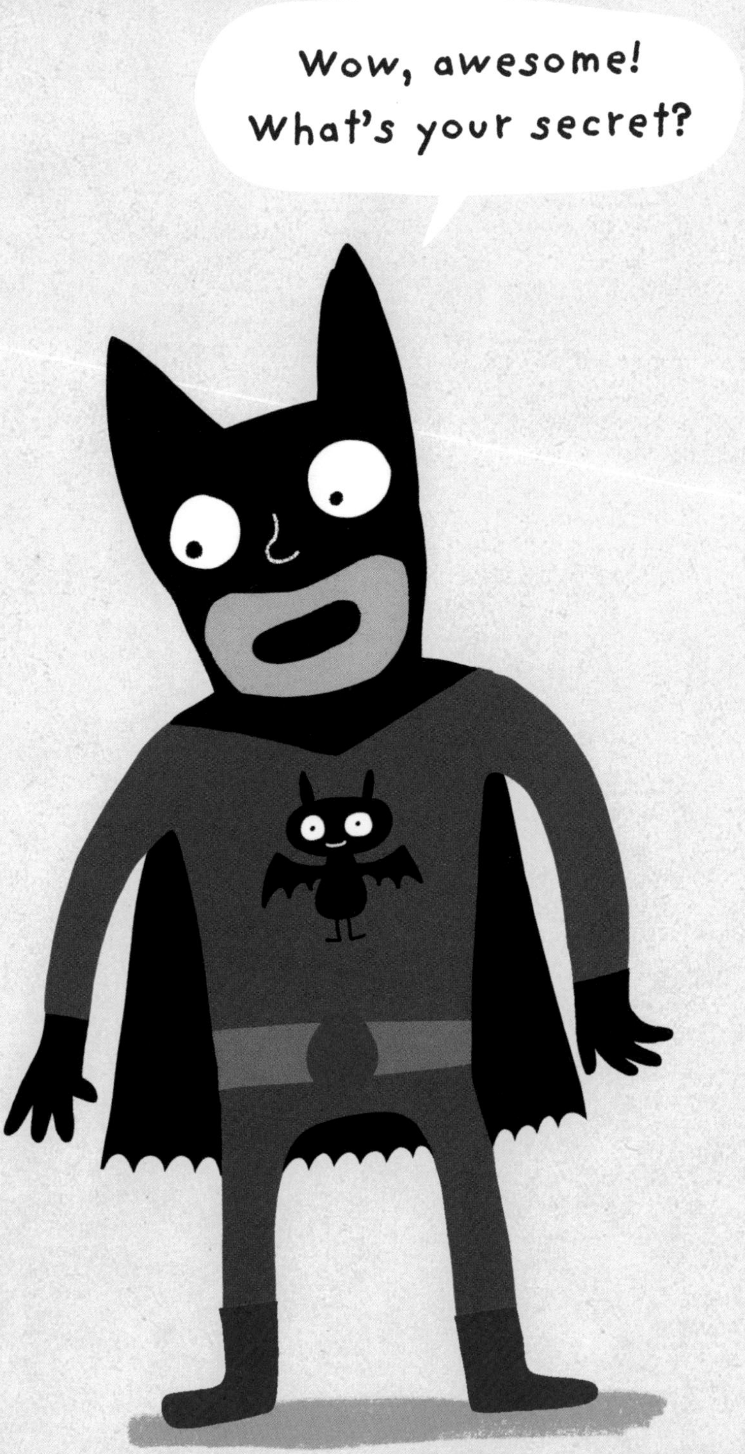
Wow, awesome!
What's your secret?

The bat is kind of

SCARY

to some people, but he isn't dangerous.
However, if he's disturbed, he may bite
to defend himself and could transmit
diseases. It's best not to touch the bat
if you come across him.

I don't really want to
bite you! Humans taste
yucky. I prefer flies.

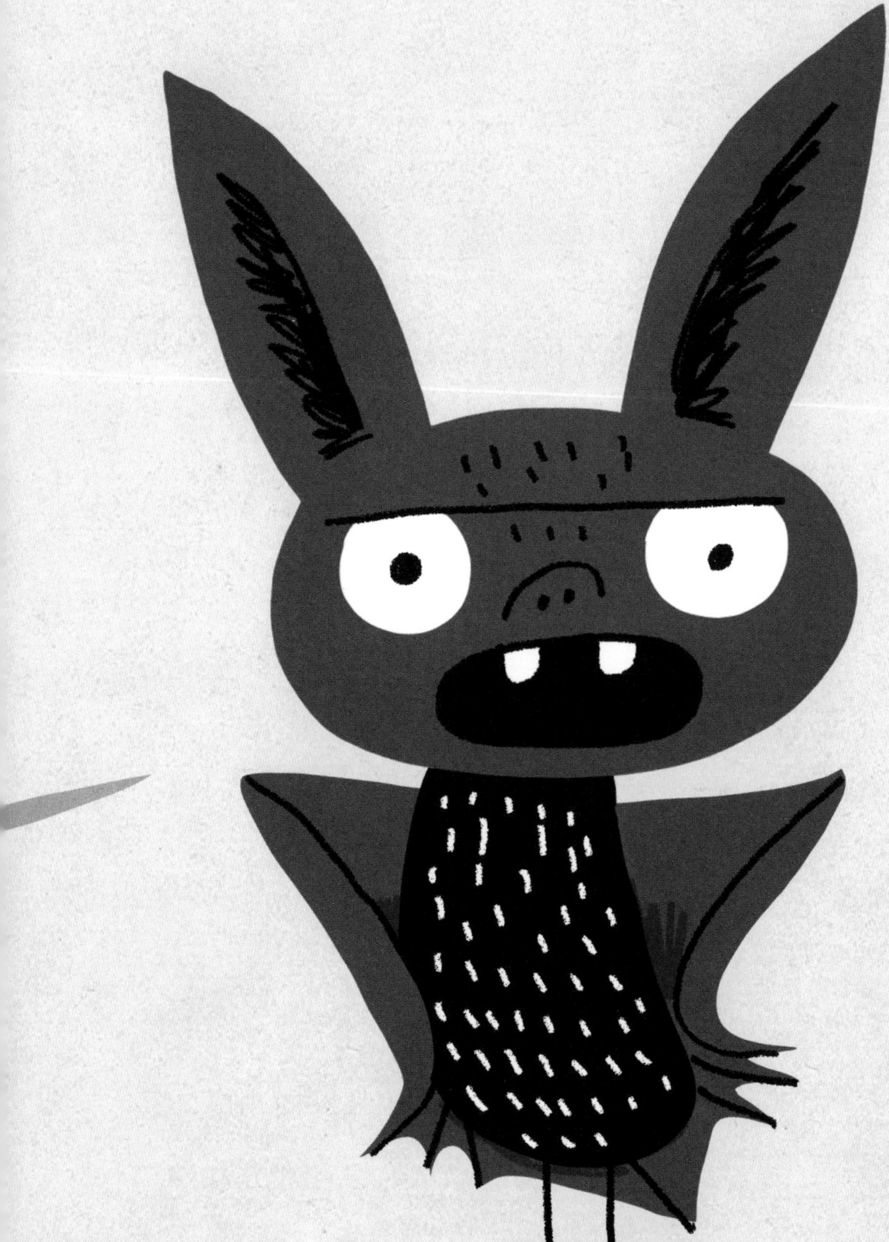

The bat plays a very important role in

NATURE.

Bats that eat fruit help pollinate flowers. And those that eat pesky insects protect harvests so that farmers can use fewer pesticides.

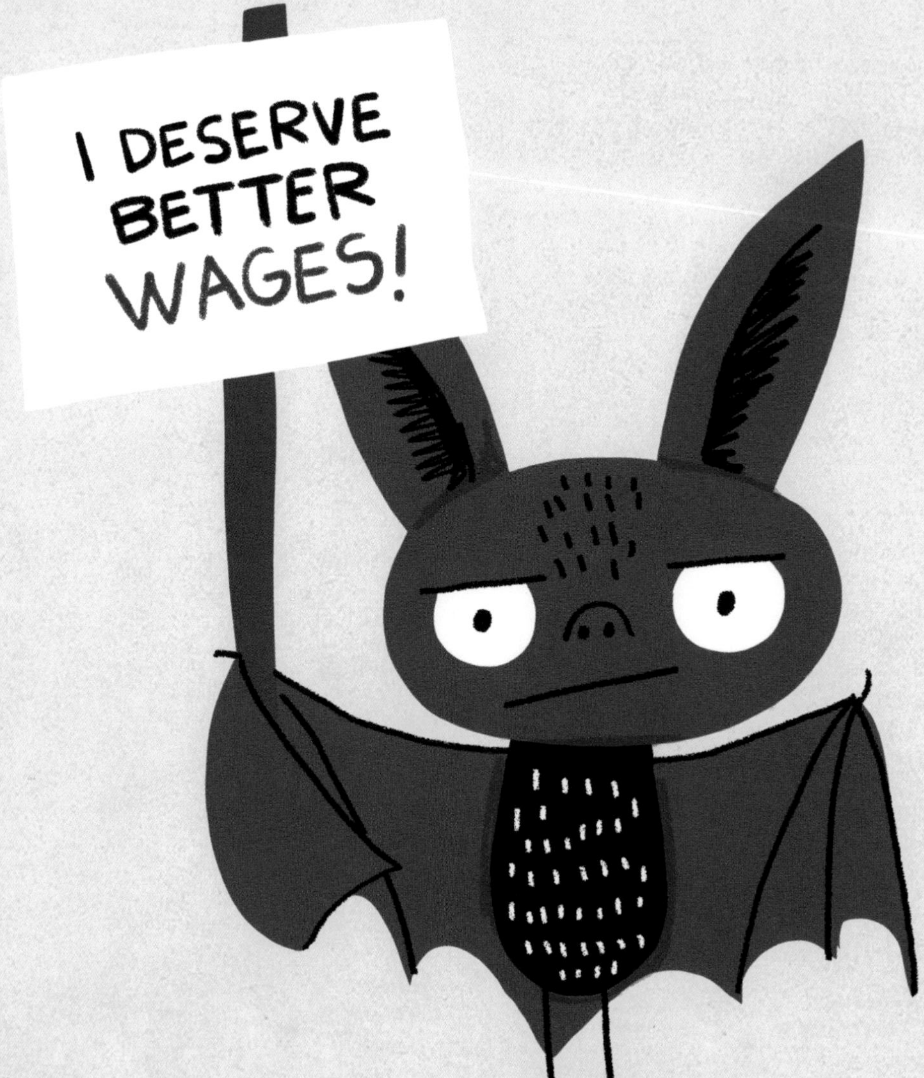
I DESERVE
BETTER
WAGES!

Unfortunately, many bats are threatened by

EXTiNCTioN.

To protect them, we have to stop destroying their habitats or start creating places for them to live and hibernate undisturbed.

BOOM!

BANG!

CRASH!

HAHAHA!

POW!

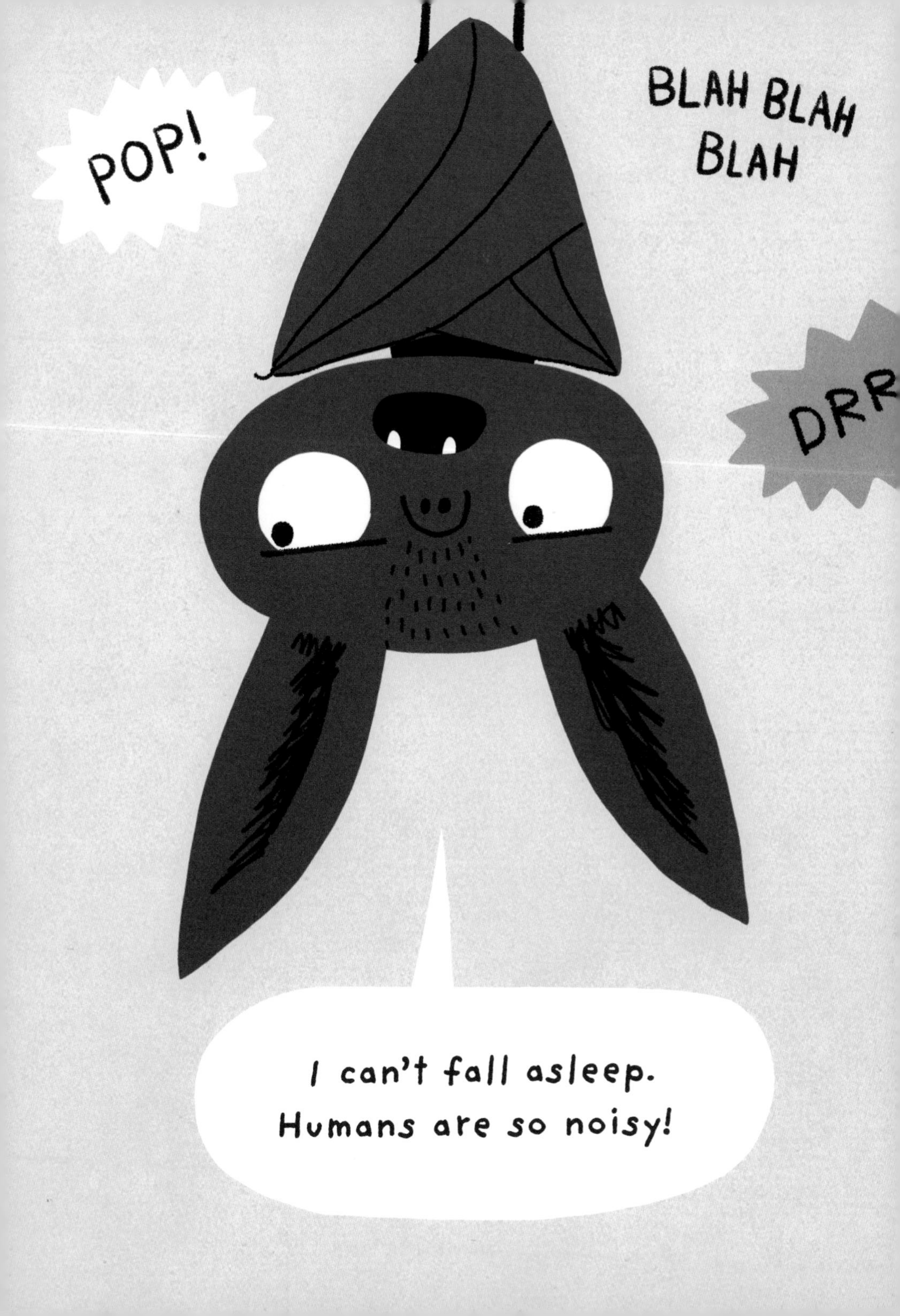
POP!
BLAH BLAH BLAH
DRR
I can't fall asleep. Humans are so noisy!

So next time you see a bat, just let him snore away

IN PEACE.

The bat is your friend!

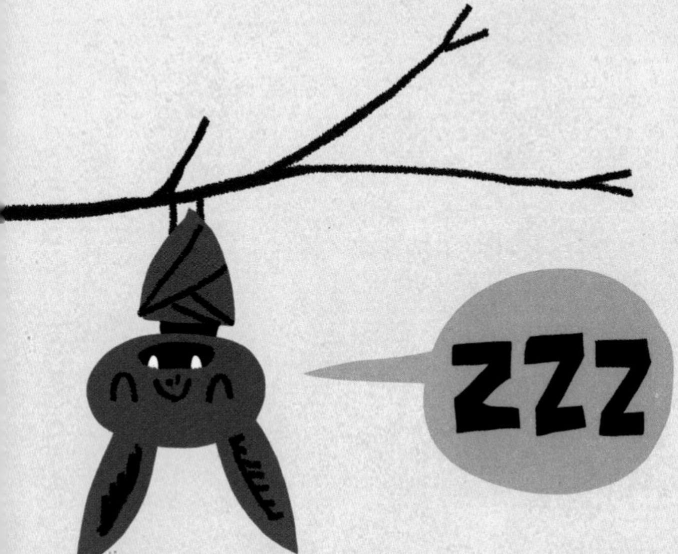
ZZZ

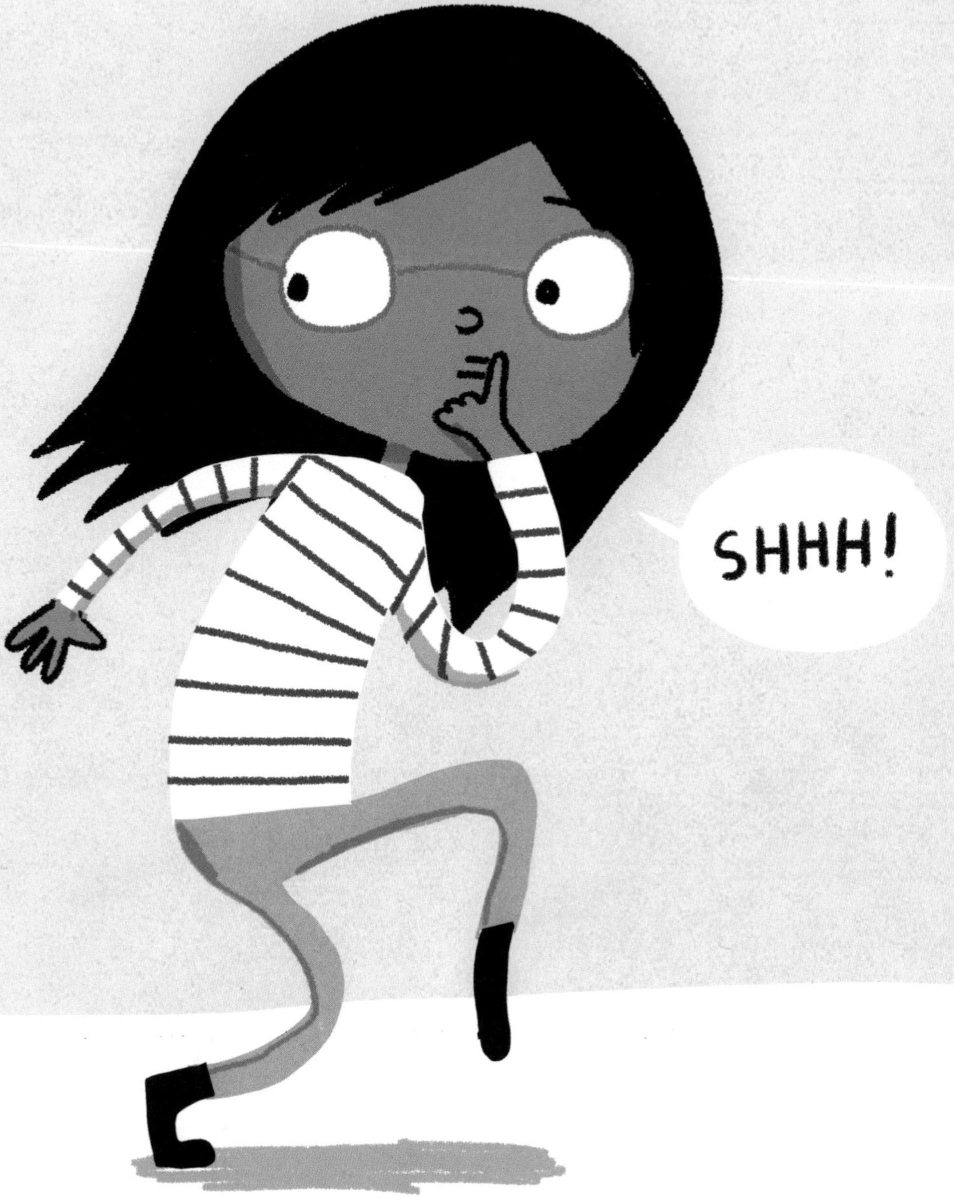
SHHH!